There are several spices, vegetables, fruits and other sources to maintain a healthy lifestyle. These sources of foods are rich in vitamins, protiens, carbohydrates and other essential nutrients. Spices have also numerous unexplored healing powers in their own way, but how many people are really aware of these valuable medicinal sources! In this book, you will find some valuable curative properties for every small or big diseases.

Improve Your Health

with the new series

By Dr. Rajeev Sharma

Price: Rs. 40/- Each

Vegetables

Fruits & Flowers

Honey

Spices

Apple, Guava & Mango

Carrot, Radish & Ginger

Dry Fruits & Medicinal Plants

Dairy Products & Juices

Lemon & Indian Hog Plum

Papaya & Bengal Quince

Wheatgrass & Grains

Garlic & Onion

Trees & Plants

Turmeric & Alum

Basil & Margosa

THE BOOK FACTORY

X-30, Okhla Industrial Area, Phase-II, New Delhi-110020,
Phone: 011-51611861, Fax: 011-51611866,
E-mail info@diamondpublication.com, Website: www.diamondpublication.com

Improve your Health With
SPICES

Dr. Rajeev Sharma

ISBN : 81-288-1118-5

© Publisher

Publisher	:	**The Book Factory**
		231, Sector-15A
		Noida (U.P.)
Phone	:	011-41611861
Fax	:	011-41611866
E-mail	:	sales@diamondpublication.com
Website	:	www.dpb.in
Distributed by	:	India Book Distributors (Bombay) ltd.
		New Majestic Shopping Centre,
		Basement 2, 19 & 20,
		Sir Jaggannath Shankar Seth Marg,
		Girgaum, Mumbai-400 004
		Ph. : 23829508, 23879421
		E-mail : fhead@vsnl.net
Edition	:	2006
Price	:	Rs. 50/-
Printed by	:	Adarsh Printers, Shahdara, Delhi-110032

Improve Your Health With Spices   **Rs. 50/-**
by *Rajeev Sharma*

PREFACE

Ayurveda is an ancient age old science which has helped the human beings a lot. In different ayurvedic texts, several home remedies are described with their medicinal properties.

There are several fruits such as apple, pomegranate, banana; vegetables like onion, garlic, radish, carrot, ginger; cereals; plants; honey; dairy products; water; wheat grass; spices that help enhance our life immensely. These are regular items which we find around us but most of us are unaware about properties of these nutritional substances. Balanced and healthy food itself is a key to good health.

The main aim of this series is to make general readers aware of these helpful healthy items, to which most of us are ignorant.

I have included those properties of each substance, which are scientifically proved and are prevalent in our families through the times of our forefathers. Hopefully, you will find this series beneficial for the whole family. You can choose any one of these books depicting your choice and follow one formula only, at a time. If there is any need, you can consult an ayurvedic physician or can write to me.

With thanks and regards,

Dr. Rajeev Sharma,
AAROGYA JYOTI®
320-322, Teachers Colony,
Bulandshahr(U.P.)-203001
Email-sharmarajeev108@rediffmail.com,
doctorrajeev108@indiatimes.com

CONTENTS

1. Medicinal Properties of Spices 9
   - Asafoetida 9
   - Bishop's Weed Seed 16
   - Coriander Seed 22
   - Cumin Seeds 29
   - Cloves 34
   - Salt 38
   - Turmeric 47
   - Caraway 57
   - Celery 57
   - Fennel 58
   - Genugreek 60
   - Red Pepper 61
   - Black Pepper 62

- ♦ Cinnamon 63
- ♦ Long Pepper 64
- ♦ Nutmeg 65
- ♦ Small Cardamom 66
- ♦ Tamala 68
- ♦ Indian Mustard 68
- ♦ Alum 70
2. Low Calorie Slimming Recipes 72
3. Diet Cure and Recipes for High B.P. Patients 76
4. Diet Cure for Hypertension 87
5. Magic of Water 90
6. Narcotics/Smoking/Alcohol/Ageing 92
7. Calories, Height-Weight and Essential Nutrients Tables 96

MEDICINAL PROPERTIES OF SPICES

ASAFOETIDA

Asafoetida is an expectorant, carminative, stimulant and powerful antispasmodic, antiseptic, germicidal, diuretic, laxative, antiphlegmatic, anti-flatulent, stimulator, germicidal, blood-purifier, painkiller and tonic.

Medicinal Properties

Indigestion and Stomach Problems

(i) Taking 2 gms of Hingasthak churna (Grind Bishop's weed, black-pepper, sendha namak, Peepal, Kala Jeera, dry ginger and Asafoetida roasted in ghee and a little edible soda) after meal with lukewarm water cures all digestive problems.

(ii) Taking 1 tsp of Hingashthak churna with 1 tsp of ground aniseed with water cures uneasiness due to flatulence.

(iii) Taking lemon juice, ginger juice with little roasted Asafoetida powder and sendha namak in cold water provides quick relief in flatulence.

(iv) Taking hot Asafoetida water (Asafoetida boiled in 250 ml water till it is reduced to half) releases wind and gives relief in pain.

(v) Applying a solution of Asafoetida in hot water near the navel region or taking roasted ground Asafoetida with any eatable activates appetite and eliminates digestive problems.

(vi) Taking one teaspoon of powder (made from grinding roasted Asafoetida, choti harar, sendha namak, Bishop's weed in equal quantity) twice a day cures indigestion.

(vii) Taking little Asafoetida mixed in water eliminates stomach uneasiness and wind.

Bite of Poisonous Insects

(i) Applying the paste of ground Asafoetida with water eliminates poison.

(ii) Applying a little Asafoetida mixed with Ghee on the affected part after pressing the poisoned blood to ooze out is an antidote of poison.

(iii) Applying the Asafoetida boiled in coconut milk (extracted from grated fresh coconut) on the affected part keeping it wet for a few minutes will give relief.

Stomachache in Children
(i) Applying a paste of roasted Asafoetida in ghee cures taut stomach of the child.
(ii) Rubbing Asafoetida (dissolved in water) on the upper stomach cures stomachache of the children.

Constipation
Taking Hingasthak Churna, Harar with sweet soda activates the movement of bowels.

Hiccoughs
Taking a pinch of Asafoetida with banana or gud cures hiccoughs.

Headache
Applying the solution of Asafoetida in water on the head relieves pain.

Pain in Ribs
Applying the solution of Asafoetida (in water) on the ribs eliminates pain.

Toothache
Keeping a pinch of Asafoetida on the tooth relieves pain and also destroys tooth-worms.

Foul breath
Taking Hingasthak churna with food or with warm water cures all digestive problems and then clears the foul smell of breath.

Cold and Cough
(i) Smelling the solution of little Asafoetida with water eliminates the deposited phlegm.
(ii) Taking Asafoetida roasted in ghee forces down the trapped phlegm which gets cleared by the bowel movement.

Hoarse Throat
(i) Gargling with hot water with little Asafoetida dissolved in it restores normal voice.
(ii) Sucking a small piece of fresh ginger with Asafoetida powder sprinkled on it releases all trapped phlegm and makes the voice normal.

Bronchitis
Taking water with Munakka and little Asafoetida boiled in it eliminates trouble caused by irritation of bronchial chords.

Pneumonia
(i) Taking little Asafoetida dissolved in water provides quick relief in congestion.
(ii) Massaging the chest with oil (made by roasting ground

Asafoetida and 4-5 cloves of garlic in oil) and covering it with some cloth eliminates congestion.

Arthritis
(i) Massaging the affected part with oil (boil Asafoetida, garlic and sendha namak in equal proportion in mustard oil and strain it.) and covering it with soft cloth eliminates stiffness and pain.
(ii) Taking 1 cup of hot milk in which half a spoonful of this oil is added before sleep is also very helpful.

Hysteria
Smelling Asafoetida cures hysteria.

Wounds
(i) Applying Asafoetida solution on the wound eliminates pain and cures the wound easily.
(ii) Regular intake of Asafoetida Mother Tincture (Homeopathic medicine) cures all types of wounds.

Urticaria
Applying little Asafoetida fried in ghee on the affected part helps in curing urticaria.

Low Blood Pressure
Taking roasted ground Asafoetida with water helps in curing blood pressure.

Weak Heart

(i) Taking roasted Asafoetida with water provides energy to heart, and purifies blood.

(ii) Taking little churna (Grind finely 5 gms. of Heera Asafoetida, 12 munnakkas without seeds, 12 dried dates without stones, dalchini and small cardamom-10 gms each mixed with little sendha namak, strain and store it) taken 3-4 times a day strengthens the heart.

Obesity

Taking low calories food with Asafoetida powder sprinkled on it dissolves excess fat in the body.

Diarrhoea

Taking 1 tsp churna (Roast mango seed and take out its soft part and roast Asafoetida also. Grind both with a little Sendha namak) stops loose motions.

Dysentery

Roast aniseed and Asafoetida separately in ghee and grind. Taking this powder with water cures mucous and blood coming in stool.

Worms

(i) Giving pinch of Asafoetida to children is preventive against worms and helps in throwing out the dead worms, if any.

(ii) Applying the Asafoetida solution in water by cotton wool on rectum destroys worms (as sometimes they are seen coming from rectum).

(iii) Giving enema of Asafoetida is very useful in throwing out worms.

Urinary problems

Taking little roasted Asafoetida dissolved in water cures burning sensation in urine.

Menstrual Disorders

Taking Asafoetida during menses cures menstrual disorders, increases menstrual flow and relieves of excessive pain during the periods.

Anus-itching in children

(i) Making the child drink solution of water with little Asafoetida twice a day provides relief in itching.

(ii) Pouring Asafoetida water with cotton wool externally also provides instant relief.

Delivery pains

Swallowing little Asafoetida (size of Baira) kept in piece of gud with one or two sips of water helps in quick delivery.

BISHOP'S WEED SEED (BISHOP'S WEED)

Bishop's weed is pungent and bitter in taste. It is a great stimulant, carminative, antispasmodic, germicidal, antiseptic, digestive, anti-flatulent, stimulant, diuretic, anti-pyritic, expectorant and an extraordinary tonic. The fruit combines the powerful and stimulant qualities of capsicum, bitter property of Chlretta and anti-spasmodic qualities of Asafoetida.

MEDICINAL PROPERTIES

Flatulence, Indigestion, Low Appetite

As an antispasmodic, regular use of Bishop's weed is recommended.

(i) Take -½ tsp Aqua Ptychotis (Sat) of Bishop's weed 'mixed with water in the morning and evening.

(ii) Take 1 tsp of mixture (made of 4 tsp Aqua Ptychotis with 4 tsp Lemon juice and 5 drops of Ilayachi Ark) thrice a day.

(iii) Take 1 tsp of churna (prepared with ground Bishop's weed and small Harr in equal quantity, little Asafoetida and salt to taste) with hot water after meal.

(iv) Swallow 3 gms of ground Bishop's weed with 3/4 gms of kala namak twice a day.

(v) Take 1 tsp of churna (made of Bishop's weed, black pepper, saunth taken in equal quantity) morning and evening with water.

(vi) Take Bishop's weed seeds soaked in lime juice after meal. This helps in curing digestion.

Strangury

Taking 2 gms of Bishop's weed with 3 gms of mishri twice or thrice a day relieves strangury.

Polyuria

1 tsp powder of Bishop's weed and gud in equal quantity taken 4 times a day relieves polyuria and cures pain in kidneys.

Bronchitis and Asthma

(i) Taking 1 tsp Bishop's weed with hot water in the morning and evening lessens sputum.

(ii) Fomentation of chest with hot seeds tied as poultice lessens sputum.

Cold and Cough

(i) Rubbing the palm with 6 gms of Bishop's weed tied in a cloth and smelling it repeatedly cures cold.

(ii) Drinking hot water after chewing little Bishop's weed cures cough.

(iii) Taking 1 tsp Aqua Ptychotis with little salt relieves constant cough.
(iv) Chewing betel leaf with Bishop's weed at night before going to bed controls and cures dry coughing.

Influenza
(i) Drinking boiled water with 3 gms Bishop's weed and 3 gms dalchini for 3 to 4 days thrice a day cures influenza.
(ii) Drinking decoction (made with 2-3 gms Bishop's weed boiled in 3 cups of water till a cup remains) 4 times a day for 2-3 days cures influenza.

Diarrhoea and stomachache
(i) Take Bishop's weed and salt in the ratio of 2:1 with hot water. It cures stomachache, improves digestion and controls diarrhoea.
(ii) Take 1 tsp of churna of Bishop's weed, sendha namak, black pepper, ilaichi and roasted small Harr (1 gm. each) after meal.
(iii) Take 1 gm powder (made with 15 gms Bishop's weed, 5 gms kala namak and ½ gm Asafoetida) with hot water twice a day.
(iv) Take little Bishop's weed with camphor with water twice a day.

Toothache
Give smoke to the aching tooth by burning Bishop's weed

on fire and after 2 hours (of smoke) gargle with lukewarm water (prepared by boiling 1 tsp ground Bishop's weed with little salt) twice or thrice a day. It cures toothache.

Earache

Pouring one or two drops of Bishop's weed oil helps to cures earache.

Heartache

Taking 1 tsp Bishop's weed with water stimulates the heart and cures heartache.

Throat-ache

Gargling with lukewarm Bishop's weed water (made by boiling 1 tsp. ground Bishop's weed with little salt in water) twice or thrice cures coarseness and pain in throat.

Rheumatic pains, Arthritis
  (i) Poultice of crushed Bishop's weed applied to painful rheumatic joints relieves pain.
  (ii) Massageing the affected portion with Bishop's weed oil relieves pain.

Foul Ulcers, Ringworm, Itching
  (i) Taking Bishop's weed flower (in little quantity) acts as an antiseptic and kill germs.
  (ii) Cleaning the affected part with Bishop's weed water kills the germs.

Improve Your Health With Spices

(iii) Applying the paste of Bishop's weed ground with hot water helps in curing ringworm, itching and removes offensive smell from foul ulcers.

Stomach worms

(i) Taking 3 to 7 drops of Bishop's weed oil for a few days destroys worms in stomach.

(iii) Boil 25 gms ground Bishop's weed soaked overnight in 500 ml water till 125 ml water remains. Taking this decoction (as 1 dose) twice a day for 2-3 days destroys worms. The same is to be divided and given in 2 doses for children.

Bile

Taking 2 gms of Bishop's weed with 3 gms of gud in winter season cures bile.

Menstrual disorders and post-natal care

(i) 6 gms churna of Bishop's weed with hot milk regulates the menstrual flow of blood.

(ii) Eating laddoo of Bishop's weed (Soak-washed, dried ground desi Bishop's weed in Desi Ghee for 1-2 weeks. Fry 1 kg Suji in pure ghee (250 gms Bishop's weed and khand to taste) after delivery.

(iii) Taking ground Bishop's weed with gud after delivery for a

few days relieves back-ache, cleans the uterus, stimulates digestion, increases appetite and gives strength.

Leucorrhoea

Taking the paste of Bishop's weed (25 gms soaked in 125 ml of water in earthen pot overnight and ground with water) in the morning for sometime controls leucorrhoea.

Female Infertility

(i) Taking the paste of Bishop's weed (5 gms of Bishop's weed and 25 gms mishri soaked in 125 ml water in earthen pot overnight-ground like thandal paste) with water for 8-10 days in the morning (starting from 1st day of menses) and

(ii) Having *mung ki dal* (without salt and chapattis in meals helps in curing infertility)

Pimples

Applying the paste of 30 gms or ground Bishop's weed mixed with 25 gms curd on the face at night and washing the face in the morning with hot water cures pimples and brings glow to the face.

Urticaria

Taking 1 gm ground Bishop's weed with 3 gms of gud relieves urticaria.

Stones
Taking 3-4 gms of Bishop's weed daily for sometime with water helps in breaking the stones and its expulsion from kidney or urinary bladder.

Wind
Taking 1 tsp ground Bishop's weed with ¼ tsp kaala namak in skimmed curd cures wind.

Whooping cough
Taking 1 gm paste (made by mixing ground 20 gms Bishop's weed 5 gms kaala namak in 60-70 gms honey) 3 or 4 times regularly helps in curing whooping cough.

As Deodorant
(i) Bishop's weed is very effective in killing germs and insects and purifying the air.
(ii) Keeping Bishop's weed in a cloth in cupboard infested with cockroaches or insects in curing them.

Apart from its inherent medicinal properties Bishop's weed is cheap and easily available in every kitchen. Its regular use is very beneficial and does not result in any mental or physical side effects.

CORIANDER SEED (DHANIA)
This is a great flavouring agent, stimulant, carminative, helps

in stomachache and griping pain, tranquiliser, germicidal, diuretic, anti-pyretic, curtails excessive requirement of water in digestive system and is a tonic.

Medicinal Properties

Asthma, cough (dry)
(i) Taking 1 tsp of dhania powder and mishri in boiled rice-water thrice a day controls cough.

(ii) 1 tsp Dhania sharbet mixed with 1 tsp honey thrice a day cures dry cough (Soak 50 gms coarsely ground dhania in 500 ml water overnight. Boil till decoction is 125 ml. Strain it through cloth and prepare sharbet with 250 gms sugar).

Frequent Sneezing
Smelling fresh coriander leaves stops frequent sneezing.

Diarrhoea, Indigestion
(i) 1 tsp of dhania Churna (10 gms dhania, 10 gms ilaichi and 10 gms jeera-fried and powdered) after meal controls diarrhoea, cures indigestion and increases appetite.

(ii) 1 tsp of heated powdered dhania with water checks loose motions.

(iii) 5 gms heated powdered dhania with curd or skimmed curd or water every 4 hours is useful.

(iv) ½ tsp dhania powder with little kala namak after meal helps to cure Diarrhoea, Indigestion.

(v) ½ tsp of mixture (60 gms dry dhania powder 25 gms black pepper and 25 gms salt) with water after meal cures tendency to go to toilet after meal.

Dysentery

1 tsp of decoction of dhania powder and mishri (10 gms each) thrice a day cures dysentery.

Wind

(i) 1 tsp dried dhania powder boiled in 1 cup water taken twice a day controls gaseous problems.

(ii) Oil of dhania is carminative and used in flatulent colic.

Loss of Appetite

(i) Taking 30 ml juice of fresh Coriander leaves daily increases appetite.

(ii) 1 tsp of ground powder (Coriander, small ilaichi and black pepper in equal quantity) mixed with 1 tsp ghee and sugar eliminates dyspepsia.

Giddiness, Vomiting, Nausea

Coriander boiled in water mixed with mishri eliminates nausea, giddiness and vomitting in pregnancy.

Headache

Applying the juice of fresh Coriander leaves on forehead cures headache.

Mental Weakness

Boil 125 gms ground Coriander in 500 ml water till 125 ml remains. Then, mix 125 gms mishri in it till it gets thick. Taking it regularly cures mental weakness.

Throat-ache

(i) Chewing 1 gm Coriander seeds slowly 3 or 4 times a day.

(ii) 1 tsp of Coriander with 1 tsp of mishri 4 times a day relieves throat-ache.

Stomachache

2 tsp Coriander Sharbet or 2 tsp Coriander boiled in 1 cup of water taken twice or thrice a day cures stomachache.

Malaria

½ tsp of Coriander powder with 1 tsp dried ginger thrice a day cures fever.

Heat stroke

(i) Soak 100 gms ground Coriander in 500 ml water for 1 hour in a new earthen pot. Strain it and take ½ cup water with 5 batashas every 3 hours. It cures giddiness, vomiting, nausea due to heat.

(ii) 1 tsp Coriander soaked in 1 cup water with sugar acts as preventive against heat stroke.

Blisters in Mouth
(i) Applying the ground Coriander or juice of fresh leaves on blisters cures them.
(ii) Gargling with Coriander boiled water cures blisters in mouth.

Kanthamala
(i) The Paste of Coriander and barley flour in equal quantity cures Kanthamala.
(ii) The Paste of fresh Coriander leaves with gram flour and Gulab Jal applied daily cures Kanthamala.

Bite of Poisonous Insects
Taking some Coriander seeds with cold water and applying the fresh Coriander juice mixed with vinegar cures the stinging sensation.

Night-discharge
(i) Taking 4 gms Coriander powder mixed with mishri with fresh water in the morning for 7 days cures night-discharge.
(ii) Taking 1 tsp of fresh Coriander paste with mishri and cold water in the morning cures night-discharge.
(iii) 1 tsp of Coriander powder and sugar with water in the morning and evening prevents night-discharge.

(**Note:** Don't eat anything for 1 hour after this dose.)

(iv) Coriander powder mixed with mishri in cold water taken before sleep cures this.

Baldness

Apply the juice of fresh leaves on the head makes hair glow.

Piles

(i) Coriander juice with mishri cures blood oozing from piles.

(ii) 2 tsp Coriander (fried in little ghee) and 2 tsp sugar boiled in 500 ml milk taken hot in place of tea or coffee for sometimes cures piles.

Eyesight

Taking 1 tsp of paste of Coriander leaves or 1 tsp Coriander mixed with Indian hog plum helps to improve eyesight.

Insomnia

(i) The Paste of Coriander leaves with sugar taken in water induces sleep.

(ii) Application of juice of fresh leaves on forehead is also useful.

(iii) 20 or 30 gms sharbet (by boiling fresh Coriander leaves and mishri in same quantity) daily induces sleep.

(iv) 3 to 5 gms of powder with Gulabjal (made by mixing Coriander powder, khaskhas, Binole seeds 10 gms each with 20 gms khand).

Menstrual Disorders
(i) Coriander powder with boiled rice water cures excessive bleeding during menses.//
(ii) Boil 20 gms Coriander in 200 ml water till the water reduces to 50 ml. Taking the mixture with mishri cures excessive bleeding.

Strangury
(i) Soak 30 gms half ground Coriander in 50 ml boiling water in an earthen pot overnight. After straining it in the morning mix 30 gms Batasha.//
(ii) 8-10 gms of this taken 4-5 times a day for sometime cures strangury.

Bleeding through Nose (Epistaxis)
(i) Applying the paste of fresh leaves on forehead and smelling juice of fresh leaves stops nose-bleeding due to heat.//
(ii) Taking the paste of Coriander (soaked overnight) in the morning is also useful.

General Tonic
Juice of 100 ml fresh Coriander leaves taken daily is a source of all vitamins.

Note: Fresh Coriander leaves, as flavouring agent, should be used in raw form to prevent loss of Vitamins caused by heating or boiling.

CUMIN SEEDS (JEERA)

Cumin seeds is dry, a bit astringent, carminative, stomachic, aromatic, blood-purifier. It is stimulant used in dyspepsia, diarrhoea, fever swelling, uterus problems and is germicidal insecticide.

Medicinal Properties

Mouth Ailments
- (i) Eating roasted cumin seeds eliminates foul smell in the mouth.
- (ii) Gargling with ground cumin seeds put in water with crushed ilaichi eliminates foul smell and cures blisters in the mouth.
- (iii) Applying the powder of ground roasted cumin seeds and sendha namak (in equal quantity) on the gums-and then, leaving the saliva to ooze out helps in reducing the swelling of gums and cures the pain.

Indigestion and stomach problems
- (i) Taking cumin seeds water (Take 1 tsp cumin seeds boiled in 1 glass of water, cool and strain it. Make 3 doses of it) thrice a day eliminates indigestion.
- (ii) Taking 1 tsp of churna (Grind cumin seeds, dried ginger, sendha namak, pippali, black pepper in equal quantity. Store

it in a bottle) with water after meal is a digestive which stimulates hunger. It eliminates wind and gas.

(iii) Taking ground cumin seeds with honey or Jaggery after meal cures stomachache.

Diarrhoea

(i) Taking roasted ground cumin seeds powder mixed with 1 tsp honey controls loose motions.

(ii) Taking roasted ground cumin seeds in whey after meal checks diarrhoea.

Stranguary

Taking ground cumin seeds with honey helps in controlling urine problems.

Leucorrhoea

Taking ground roasted cumin seeds with sugar controls leucorrhoea.

Post-Delivery problems

(i) Taking water in which cumin seeds powder is mixed acts as an antiseptic and helps in shrinking of ovaries to their normal size.

(ii) Taking this cumin seeds water is useful in other problems of menses after delivery.

(iii) Eating vegetables with cumin seeds fried in oil increases the quantity of milk in the breasts.

Improve Your Health With Spices

(iv) Taking 10 gms of roasted cumin seeds and sugar with 100 ml milk also increases the milk in the breasts.

(v) Taking chapatis made of dough in which cumin seeds and Bishop's weed have been kneaded helps the mother to get enough milk in her breasts.

(vi) Taking decoction made of cumin seeds just after delivery stimulates the uterus to contract to its original position.

(vii) Taking cumin seeds with gud is very beneficial for uterus contraction.

Piles

(i) Taking cumin seeds with mishri helps in curing piles.

(ii) Taking 1 cup water (Boil-cumin seeds, saunf, Coriander seeds 1 tsp each in a glass of water till one cup is left) with pure ghee eliminates oozing of blood in piles.

(iii) Taking 1 tsp ground cumin seeds and 1 tsp ground black pepper with honey eliminates pain and cures piles.

Urticaris

Taking bath with water having cumin seeds boiled in it cures urticaria and itching.

Spots, freckles

(i) Applying the paste (made from ground cumin seeds, sesame seeds, and mustard in equal quantity mixed in milk) on face eliminates spots and freckles and imparts a natural softness and glow.

(ii) Washing the face with water in which cumin seeds is boiled beautifies the skin.

Chronic Fever

(i) Taking cumin seeds with gud twice a day for 3 weeks cures chronic fever.

(ii) Taking 3-4 gms of churna of cumin seeds (Boil cumin seed in Cow's milk-when dried-grind it) with mishri regularly cures chronic fever.

Swelling of hands and feet

Applying the paste of cumin seeds powder with water removes painful swelling of hands and feet.

Hoarse throat

Gargles with cumin seeds water eliminates hoarseness of throat.

Insect-bite

(i) Applying a paste of cumin seeds and dried ginger on the affected part (in case of spider bite) eliminates the poison.

(ii) Taking ground cumin seeds and black pepper in water (in case of dog-bite) eliminates poison.

(iii) Applying the heated paste of ground cumin seeds with

sendha namak and butter/oil in case of scorpion bite eliminates poison.

Worms

Taking 1 tsp cumin seeds with water before going to bed for 2 or 3 days kills the worms.

Insect-repellent

(i) Keeping a little bundle of cumin seeds in cupboards makes them free from insects.

(ii) Keeping cumin seeds between woollen shawls and clothes acts as a protection against insects.

General Tonic

(i) Taking 2-3 gms of ground cumin seeds boiled in 100 ml of water for 5 minutes with milk and add sugar to taste provides energy and vigour to the whole body.

(ii) Eating kheer of 20 gms cumin seeds (soak cumin seed in 250 ml milk for 2 hours. Cook on slow fire, till it is thickened. Mix sugar or mishri according to taste) stimulates digestion and strengthens physical and mental faculties.

Precaution

Pregnant ladies should not take cumin seeds in excessive quantity as it may lead to 'ABORTION'.

CLOVES

Clove is aromatic anti-emetic, local anaesthetic and antiseptic. It is carminative, anti-gastric, pain killer and anti-pyreutic.

Medicinal properties

Indigestion, Diarrhoea Flatulence

(i) Taking 2 or 3 drops of cloves Oil in sugar cures indigestion, intestinal problems and also diarrhoea.

(ii) Taking cloves as flavouring agent corrects griping caused by purgative and cures flatulence.

(iii) Taking cloves in combination with other spices and sendha namak relieves indigestion, vomiting and quenches thirst.

(iv) Taking two ground cloves put in warm water eliminates nausea, gas and indigestion.

(v) Chewing clove is also useful in nausea.

(vi) Chewing a clove twice after meal or taking it in Sherbet cures all acidic problems.

(vii) Taking clove in betel leaf or 1/4 tsp ground cloves, little rock salt with lukewarm water after meal cures flatulence.

(viii) Taking a clove lightly roasted in ghee after meal releases all trapped wind in the body.

(ix) Taking 1 gm cloves churna (made by grinding cloves, dried

ginger, Bishop's weed and sendha namak 3 gms each) twice a day cures all digestive problems and increases appetite.

Headache

(i) Applying the paste of cloves or cloves-oil curves headache.

(ii) Taking 2-3 cloves water (cloves boiled in 1 cup water till half is left) twice a day cures headache.

Weakness after illness

Taking boiled water in which the cloves have been boiled imparts resistance to fight against infections and ailments.

Cough, Throat problems

(i) Sucking the juice of roasted cloves cures itching in the throat.

(ii) Keeping cloves in mouth releases trapped phlegm and eliminates foul smell of the mouth.

(iii) Taking a little powder of cloves and pomegranate rind (in equal quantity) mixed with honey twice or thrice a day cures coughing.

(iv) Sucking 2 cloves roasted on griddle eliminates phlegm.

Hoarseness of Throat

(i) Taking roasted ground cloves with honey provides relief to hoarseness of throat.

(ii) Chewing clove and sucking its juice soothes vocal chords.
(iii) Chewing clove with mishri is also beneficial.
(iv) Keeping the clove (roasted on the flame of a candle) in mouth eliminates foul smell of breath and cures sore-throat.

Hiccoughs

Taking water of 1-2 cloves (cloves soaked in lukewarm water) cures hiccoughs.

Influenza

Taking 1/4 tsp powdered cloves and pipali, 1/4 tsp ginger juice with 1 tsp honey 3-4 times a day provides relief.

Pneumonia

Taking betel leaf with a little cloves oil spread on it and mishri early in the morning clears congestion and brings relief.

Fever

Taking powder of 1 clove with warm water thrice a day cures fever.

Malaria

(i) Taking a clove heated in pure ghee and basil leaf early in the morning prevents Malaria.
(ii) Taking tea with clove and basil leaves boiled in it eliminates Malaria.

Typhoid
Taking clove water (boil 5 cloves in 2 lt water till 1 lt is left. Strain and cool it) is useful in curing typhoid.

Asthma
Taking 3-4 roasted cloves before going to bed eliminates congestion in the chest and gives relief in breathing.

Measles
Taking one clove rubbed with water on stone with honey provides relief.

Worms
(i) Taking clove water whenever thirsty throws out worms.
(ii) After dinner chewing one clove before eating a ripe small roasted tomato also helps in throwing out worms.

Stranguary
Taking cloves with water twice or thrice a day helps in curing this.

Ulcer
Applying the paste of cloves and turmeric cures ulcer.

Bite of Poisonous Insects
Applying the paste of cloves (rubbed with water on stone) on the affected part provides relief.

Rheumatic-pain
Applying the paste of cloves on the affected part provides relief.

Excessive thirst
Taking boiling hot water of cloves quenches excessive thirst.

Teeth care and problems
(i) Rubbing the teeth with ground cloves and lemon juice cures toothache and makes the teeth shining.
(ii) Gargling with cloves water (3-4 cloves boiled in 1 glass water) twice or thrice a day cures toothache.
(iii) Pressing cotton soaked in cloves oil on the cavity in tooth eliminates pain.
(iv) Applying the cloves-oil on the affected teeth before going to bed for somedays checks foul smell and cures Pyrrhoea.
(v) Taking roasted cloves strengthens gums and teeth.

Sty
Applying the clove rubbed on stone with water on the sty eliminates swelling.

SALT

Two varieties of salts are common:

Alkaline salt – procured from the salt of oceans, is sweet and bitter, digestive, appetiser, carminative, cures wind.

Sambhar salt – procured from Sambhar Lake in Rajasthan, is light.

Medicinal Properties

Indigestion, stomach problems

(i) Taking 5 gms black salt in hot water in the morning eliminates indigestion and improves appetite.

(ii) Taking Lavana Bhaskara churna (made from the available 5 types of salt) with warm water after meal eliminates flatulence.

(iii) Taking the oozed water of onion pieces on which sendha namak has been sprinkled after meal is very useful in curing flatulence.

(iv) Taking ginger juice with little sendha namak half an hour before meal improves appetite.

(v) Massaging the stomach with salt mixed in hot ghee cures wind and stomachache.

(vi) Taking salt in hot water cures stomachache and also helps in easy movement of bowels.

Diarrhoea

Taking ½ tsp powder of sendha namak, pipal and choti harad (in equal proportion) with water after meal twice a day cures loose motions caused by indigestion.

Dysentery

Taking whey with little sendha namak with or after meal cures dysentry.

Headache

(i) Keeping a pinch of salt on the tongue for 10 minutes and then, drinking cold water eliminates headache.

(ii) Rubbing, little salt in pure ghee on the temples provides relief in headache due to cold.

(iii) Putting one or two drops of salt water in the nostrils eliminates headache.

(iv) Smelling salt water (in 1:20 proportion) also is helpful in it.

Migraine

Licking 1 tsp salt mixed with 1 tsp honey brings relief in pain.

Baldness

Washing the head with salted water helps in hair-growth.

Dandruff

Washing the hair with salted water eliminates dandruff.

Eye-problems

(i) Washing the eyes with cold salted water (1 tsp salt in 1 lt water) cures watery discharge, and eliminates swelling.

(ii) Washing the eyes with lukewarm salted water cures trachoma.

Dental problems

(i) Rinsing the mouth regularly with salted water eliminates pain due to tooth decay.

(ii) Applying the strained salt mixed in mustard oil (kept in sun for one day) as toothpaste strengthens the gums and teeth and eliminates pyorrhoea.

(iii) Applying the strained kaala namak mixed in the oil as tooth paste strengthens the loose teeth at their base.

(iv) Applying the strained salt and peepal leaf powder with honey (in 1:3 proportion) as toothpaste for a few minutes to let the saliva ooze out is also very useful in strengthening loose teeth.

(v) Applying finely powdered sendha namak on the gums relieves pain in gums and teeth.

Boils on tongue

Applying a paste made of white mustard seeds with sendha namak and allowing the saliva to ooze out eliminates boils on the tongue.

Hoarse Voice

(i) Taking ground 10 gms of jujube (small red ones) with 2 gms sendha namak with honey twice or thrice a day cures hoarseness of voice.

(ii) Gargling with warm salted water also is useful.

Hiccoughs

(i) Drinking water with little sendha namak provides instant relief.

(ii) Smelling a piece of jaggery with little sendha namak sprinkled on it or taking a piece of Jaggery with water stops hiccoughs caused by hot and spicy food.

(iii) Taking kala and sendha namak with water and one lemon juice after meal is also useful.

Swelling and Pain

(i) Put some salt in a cloth and then heat on a griddle (also apply a little oil on it). Thereafter, fomentation will provide relief in bruise or sprain and eliminate swelling.

(ii) Massaging the swollen part with pure ghee and salt mixture provides relief.

(iii) Rinsing mouth and gargling with salted lukewarm water eliminates swelling on the neck and face.

(iv) Massaging around the joints with sendha salt roasted over fire in the sesame seeds oil eliminates swelling.

(v) Fomentation eliminates swelling due to Rheumatic fever.

Fatigue

Sitting in the tub of lukewarm water with little salt or putting feet in that water for a few minutes eliminates fatigue and imparts freshness.

Cold and Cough

(i) Taking 1 glass boiled water with sendha namak, ground

black pepper and turmeric (boil it till reduced to half) cures cold.
(ii) Dropping juice of basil with little salt in the nostrils cures cold.
(iii) Massaging the chest with salted pure ghee provides relief in cold and helps in extracting the trapped phlegm.
(iv) Sucking a piece of salt provides relief in cough.
(v) Washing the nose or gargling or smelling the salted water provides relief in cold and cough.

Asthma

Taking sendha namak and Desi Boora (1:4 ratio) with 100 ml warm water helps in curing Asthma.

Bronchitis

Massaging salted lukewarm pure ghee on the affected portion eliminates the swelling in the bronchial chords.

Influenza

Taking the paste of 5 garlic cloves and a little salt with hot basil tea helps in eliminating the germs through sweat and urine.

Arthritis

(i) Fomentation with hot water and salt on the affected part provides relief.
(ii) Massaging the affected part with mustard oil and little salt (Kept in sun for 1 day) provides relief.

(iii) Taking bath with salted warm water is also useful.

Skin-problems

(i) Massaging the body with salted mustard oil removes dryness of skin.

(ii) Applying salted pure ghee in the navel cures dryness of lips and applying it on the feet and hands cures cracked feet and hands.

(iii) Applying ginger juice with sendha namak on the affected part eliminates acnes and pimples.

(iv) Taking juice or soup with sendha namak, black pepper and lemon juice cures eruptions due to heat.

(v) Washing the affected part or taking bath with water in which husk of wheat and sendha namak (in 10:1 proportion) has been boiled and then, cooled regularly eliminates skin eruptions, cures itching and eczema.

(vi) Applying the paste of salt and water on the affected part also help in curing eczema and other skin problems.

Vomiting

(i) Taking ginger and lemon juice with sendha namak controls vomiting.

(ii) Rubbing salted ghee on stomach in clockwise direction is also very useful.

Excessive Thirst
Taking salted lime water twice or thrice a day quenches excessive thirst.

Stones
Taking sendha namak or kala namak mixed in lime juice and water twice or thrice a day helps in dissolving the stones, which then passes out through urine.

Worms
Taking banana sprinkled with sendha namak and lemon juice on empty stomach for 2-3 days kills and throws out the worms.

Piles
(i) Applying salt on the fistulas is very useful in curing piles.
(ii) Taking a little salt provides instant relief in bleeding.

Cramps
Fomentation of common salt and ground turmeric dipped in warm mustard oil on the affected part provides relief.

Menstrual Problems
Taking 2 gms of salt in warm water twice or thrice a day helps in natural flow of blood in menses.

Malaria
(i) Taking ½ tsp (for children) and 1 tsp salt (fried on griddle

till it turns golden brown) with warm water on empty stomach helps in curing Malaria.

(ii) Taking sendha namak and Desi Boora (1:4 ratio) with warm water is also very useful.

Mumps

Gargling with salted water and fomentation with salted warm water eliminates swelling.

Effect of Poison or hangover of liquor

Taking 60 gms of salt in water encourages vomiting out poisonous substance.

Insect Bite

Rubbing the affected portion with salt after pouring some water and also taking salted water eliminates irritation, pain and swelling caused by the bite of poisonous insect.

Scorpion-Bite

(i) Rubbing the affected part with half tsp garlic juice mixed with ¼ th tsp salt melts away the sting.

(ii) Dropping four drops of saturated solution (by dissolving 3-4 gms of salt in 100 ml of water) in the eyes/ears opposite the side on which the scorpion has bitten is very effective in nullifying the toxic effect.

Dog-Bite

Rubbing the mixture of ground garlic and salt over the affected portion eliminates the effect of dog-bite.

Canadian doctors have opined that, ladies wishing to have male progeny should have food with higher quantity of salt as compared to milk, cheese, butter, etc. They should start taking more salty food not only during pregnancy but 6 weeks before the conception. Salt produces potassium and sodium in the body and has great effect on chromosomes, which determine the sex of the baby.

Dr. Jacks Lorren, renowned doctor of Montreal (Canada), said that out of 296 ladies, who adopted their dietary habits according to his instruction, 265 ladies had the sex of the baby according to their choice.

(**Note:** Intake of salt should be stopped in patients suffering from hysteria, epilepsy, hypertension, kidney problems, arthritis, eczema, itching etc.).

TURMERIC

Turmeric is a stringent and sour in taste. It is a time-tested beauty aid and a nourishing herb which not only gives natural gloss, royal glow and lustre, but also imparts vigour and youthful vitality to the entire body. Turmeric is thus, a great tonic in general, aromatic, diuretic, expectorant, blood-purifier, skin-tonic, carminative, pain reliever, germicidal, anti-flatulent, producer and enhancer of red blood corpuscles, anti-phlegmatic, antibilleous, protector of eyes, anti-inflammatory and imparts coolness to the system.

Medicinal Properties

Bruises, sprain and wounds

(i) Applying the paste of turmeric powder with lime or water on the affected part eliminates swelling and pain in bruises.

(ii) Taking 1 tsp turmeric powder with hot milk is also useful.

(iii) Filling the wound or cut (from which blood is coming out) with turmeric powder will stop bleeding and cures the wound/cut.

(iv) Applying poultice made of gram flour, turmeric powder mixed with mustard or sesame oil on the sprained portion enhances blood circulation and provides relief.

(v) Tying a bandage of turmeric (prepared with 4 tsp flour, 2 tsp turmeric powder, 1 tsp pure ghee, ½ tsp sendha namak with water) on the bruised portion provides relief.

(vi) Giving fomentation with cloth soaked in hot water (500 ml water boiled with 1 tsp sendha namak and 1 tsp turmeric powder) on the bruised part eliminates pain and swelling.

(vii) Giving fomentation (having one ground onion mixed with 1 tsp. turmeric powder) heated with Sesame oil on the bruised portion provides relief.

(viii) Applying turmeric powder heated in butter-oil on the wound and tying it with a bandage helps in quick healing of the wound.

(ix) Dusting turmeric powder on wounds also helps.

Skin-problems

(i) Ringworm, white spots: Applying the paste of turmeric rubbed on stone with water on the affected portion is useful.

(ii) Skin eruptions: Applying the paste of turmeric and sesame oil on the body prevents skin eruptions.

(iii) Applying turmeric powder or the paste on the body before bath is a preventive measure against skin problems and also a depilatory substance.

(iv) Urticaria:
   (a) Taking 1 tsp turmeric powder with 1 tsp mishri or honey twice a day cures urticaria.

(b) Taking halwa (made from 2 tsp. flour, 1 tsp. ghee, 1 tsp turmeric, 2 tsp sugar, 1 cup water) in the morning cures Utricaria.

(v) Taking roasted turmeric with gud cures itching.

(vi) Eczema: Sucking tablet of ground turmeric with honey for 10- 15 days cures eczema.

(vii) Pustules: Placing cotton dipped in turmeric oil over pustules provides relief.

(viii) Freckles, spots:

(a) Applying turmeric rubbed on stone with water eliminates them.

(b) Massaging the face with Ubtan (mix ground turmeric with milk of banyan or pipal and soak it overnight) 1 hour before bath eliminates freckles on the face and imparts natural glow.

Cough & Cold, Asthma

(i) Taking turmeric powder and little salt with hot water or sucking a small piece of turmeric or licking 1 tsp turmeric powder with ¼ tsp honey provides relief in cough and eliminates congestion of bronchi.

(ii) Taking ¼ tsp turmeric with hot milk is helpful in checking running nose.

(iii) Inhaling the smoke of burnt turmeric throws out the trapped phlegm.

(iv) Taking ¼ tsp powder of turmeric (roasted in hot sand and then ground) with hot water cures breathing problem (Asthma).

(v) Taking turmeric boiled in milk and sweetened with Jaggery is very useful in cold and asthma.

(vi) Sucking a piece of turmeric (like lemon drops) or keeping it in the mouth at night cures chronic cold.

(vii) Licking tablets (made by mixing turmeric powder, barley powder and bansa-ash in equal proportion with honey and making small tablets) 4-5 times in a day eliminates trapped phlegm in the body.

(viii) Massaging the throat and chest with little turmeric powder, ground black pepper mixed with ghee cures irritation in the bronchial chords.

(ix) Giving a pinch of turmeric powder with milk to children provides quick relief.

(x) Inhaling smoke of cow-dung cake with turmeric sprinkled on it releases the trapped phlegm.

(xi) Taking ¼ tsp of turmeric powder with 3-4 gulps of warm water acts as a preventive against attack of asthma.

Whooping cough
(i) Taking 1 tsp ground roasted turmeric powder with two spoons of honey 3 or 4 times a day provides relief in cough.

(ii) Taking betel leaf with little turmeric piece in it is also useful.

Indigestion & Stomach problems
(i) Taking turmeric powder and salt in equal quantity with warm water provides instant relief in acidity.

(ii) Taking 1 tsp churna (Grind turmeric 4 gm, Dried ginger 4 gm, Black pepper 2 gms and ilaichi 2 gms) after meal is digestive and eliminates wind and stomach ailments.

(iii) Taking curd or whey with turmeric powder after lunch cures digestive problems.

Sore Throat
Licking turmeric powder mixed with honey twice or thrice a day cures soreness.

Tonsilitis
Fomentation with paste made of 10 gms turmeric powder roasted in mustard oil and then, tied around the neck provides relief in tonsils.

Blisters In mouth
Gargling with water in which little turmeric powder is boiled, twice a day, cures blisters in mouth.

Urinary Troubles
Taking the paste of ground or juice of raw turmeric and honey with goat's milk (if available) twice a day, cures all urinary problems.

Small-pox
(i) Taking 1 tsp powder of turmeric and tamarind for 4-5 days acts as a preventive against small-pox.
(ii) Applying a thin layer of the ubtan (Haldi powder, foam of fresh milk and Wheat flour mixed with mustard oil or fresh cream) on the affected part twice a day flattens the deep spots of small-pox and makes the skin soft.

Worms
Licking the paste (made of ¼ tsp turmeric powder and ½ tsp vayavidang churna with 1 tsp of honey for 7-8 days) kills worms and throws them out.

Pregnancy and postnatal care
(i) Taking 5-10 gms of turmeric powder with water during menses is an anti-pregnancy dose for ladies.
(ii) Taking 1 tsp turmeric with hot milk in latter part of the 9th month of pregnancy helps in easy delivery.
(iii) Taking 1 tsp roasted turmeric powder with gud after delivery eliminates weakness and cures uterus swelling.

Pain in breasts
Applying the paste of turmeric rubbed on stone on the affected part eliminates pain.

Gout
Taking laddoo of turmeric (mix ½ kg roasted ground turmeric, one finely grated dried coconut, 1 kg jaggery, 200 gms cashew nuts or ground nuts and make laddoo) daily in the morning with basil or lemon tea makes the joints supple and provides relief in pain and swelling.

Pain in Ribs
(i) Applying the paste of turmeric powder mixed in hot water on the aching ribs provides relief.
(ii) Massaging the ribs with turmeric oil.
(iii) Massaging the ribs with the paste of turmeric powder in milk of the calotropis plant provides quick relief.

Jaundice & Liver problems
Taking 4-5 gms of turmeric powder mixed in a glass of whey twice a day activates the liver.

Diabetes
Taking 4-5 gms ground turmeric with water or honey twice a day is helpful in curing diabetes.

Leucorrhoea

(i) Taking turmeric powder with sugar twice a day for sometime cures this.

(ii) Washing the private parts with turmeric water (10 gms turmeric boiled in 100 ml water) is also useful. Taking one Batasha with 8-10 drops of milk of Banyan tree before sunrise, along with it for 7 days helps in early cure.

Debility in Males

Taking about 7-8 gms of raw ground turmeric and equal amount of honey with goat's milk cures debility in males.

Dental Problems

(i) Rinsing the mouth with turmeric water (boil 5 gms turmeric powder, 2 cloves and 2 dried leaves of guava in 200 ml water) provides instant relief.

(ii) Applying and rubbing the teeth with the paste of turmeric powder, salt and mustard oil strengthens the gums.

(iii) Massaging the aching teeth with roasted ground turmeric eliminates pain and swelling.

(iv) Keeping piece of roasted turmeric near the aching tooth and letting the saliva ooze out also helps in curing dental problems.

(v) Filling the cavity in teeth with roasted ground turmeric powder provides relief from pain.

(vi) Applying the powder of burnt turmeric piece and Bishop's weed on teeth and cleaning them makes the gums and teeth strong.

Ear troubles

Putting one or two drops of turmeric (by roasting 2 pieces of turmeric in mustard oil) in the ear, cleaning it with an ear-bud cures ear problems.

Eye-troubles

(i) Cloth dipped in the solution of turmeric powder and water is employed as an eye-shade.

(ii) Dropping turmeric water (1 tsp turmeric powder boiled in 500 ml water till 125 ml water is left. Cool and strain it through a fine cloth) in the eyes twice a day and putting the cotton soaked in water on the eyelids cures pain, redness, irritation and itching in the eyes.

(iii) Applying bit heated paste of piece of turmeric rubbed on stone on eyelids also eliminates pain, swelling and eye-troubles.

(iv) A decoction of turmeric powder with water as a cooling lotion on the eyes is useful in conjunctivitis.

Poison of Insect bite

Applying the mixture of turmeric powder and lime over the affected part nullifies the toxic effect.

Coryza

Inhalations of fumes of burning turmeric passed into the nostrils relieves coryza.

CARAWAY

The caraway seeds contain 4.5% moisture, 7.67% proteins, 8.8% fat, 50.2% carbohydrates, 3.7% minerals matter, 25.2% fibre. They also contain vitamins B_1, B_2, C and A: Plant part used – Fruits and Seeds.

Medicinal Properties

(i) Mix caraway seeds with sugarcandy in equal amount and make a powder. Take half spoonful of powder with water in the morning and evening to cure piles.

(ii) Make a powder of the seeds. Mix one spoonful of the powder and one cup of curd. Take it twice a day for curing stomach problems.

CELERY

The celery seeds contain 5.1% moisture, 18.1% proteins, 22.8% fat, 40.9% carbohydrates, 10.2% mineral matter, 2.9% crude fibre and vitamins B_1, B_2 C and A. Plant part used– Fruits and seeds.

Improve Your Health With Spices

Medicinal Properties

- Make powder of seeds and cloves and then, mix with honey. Take the mixture to stop vomitting. Take celery seeds and place them in mustard oil. Simmer and rub the warm mixture on the sites of pain to control body pain.
- Make powder of seeds and mix black salt. Take it thrice a day to cure stomachache.
- Make powder of the seeds. Place it on the site of ache. Rub it gently over the teeth and gum. The ache will disappear soon.
- Take a few seeds with cold water early in the morning. It will keep cold away.
- Make powder of the seeds and mix with honey. Taking thrice a day for a week. It helps to reduce hypertension.

FENNEL

The fennel seeds contain 6.3 % moisture, 9.5 % proteins, 10 % fat, 42.3 % carbohydrates, 13.4 % minerals matter, 18.5 % crude fibre and vitamins B_1, B_2 C and A. Plant part used - Fruits and Seeds.

Medicinal Properties

- Fry fennel seeds and then mix black salt in equal amount.

Improve Your Health With Spices

Taking a spoonful in the morning and evening will remove the constipation and prevent indigestion.
- Prepare a juice of fennel seeds. Place a few drops in a batasha and then, take twice a day. It will remove the feeling of difficulty and pain during urination.
- Take fennel seeds after meal and chew them slowly to cure dyspepsia.
- Make a powder of seeds and mix with rind of Bengal quince or Stone Apple in equal amount. Take a spoonful with curd thrice a day to treat dysentery.
- Soak 50 gms of fennel seeds in mud pitcher for a night and take a bath in the morning. It will heal pimples and boils present in any part of the body during summer to heal pimples and boils.
- Mix fennel seeds and sugarcandy in equal amount and then, prepare a powder. Take two spoonfuls of the powder with fresh water at the night before sleep. It will improve the eyesight and will check the formation of cataract.
- Boil fennel seeds in water and then strain. Mix a spoonful of it in milk. Give it to the patient thrice a day. The child will not feel indigestion, dysentery and pain during the teething period.

FENUGREEK

Fenugreek seeds contain 9.6% moisture, 35.7 % carbohydrates, 10.4 % proteins, 15.9 % fat, 20.1 % fibre, 6.5 % mineral matter and vitamins B_1, B_2, C and A. Plant part used-Seeds.

Medicinal Properties

- Soak seeds in cold water for 5 hours and then, boil for two minutes. Take one cup per day to cure hay fever.
- Mix fenugreek seeds and dill seeds in equal amount and then, make a powder. Take two spoonfuls in the morning and evening with fresh water to control blood pressure.
- Put a little seeds in water at night. Take wet seeds orally with water twice a day to reduce cholesterol.
- Boil fenugreek seeds in milk. Cool and strain. Mix sugarcandy and then, take the mixture. It will stop bleeding from any part of the body.
- Boil the seeds and then crush them to form a paste. Mix honey, take it twice a day for one month to treat asthma.
- Make powder of the seeds. Take 5 gms regularly twice a day with water. Chances of pain in any joints of body will not occur even in old age.

- Soak two spoonfuls of fenugreek seeds in water overnight. Take them in the morning before breakfast to cure diabetes.

RED PEPPER

On an average, dried chillies contain 10 % moisture, 15.9 % proteins, 6.2 % fat, 31.6 % carbohydrates, 30.2 % fibre and 6.1 % ash. They also contain vitamins (riboflavin, niacin and ascorbic acid). The pungency is due to a crystalline phenolic substance known as, capsaicin. Plant part used–Dried ripe fruits.

Medicinal Properties

- Mix seeds of chillies and drops of lemon juice in tomato juice. Consume it regularly twice a day to lower cholesterol level.
- Grind red peppers in water to prepare a paste. Apply it directly on the dog bites. It will first check the bleeding and then will heal the injured parts.
- Consume red peppers in your diet regularly. The chances of blood clot problems are prevented.
- Consume red peppers in your diet regularly in small quantity. It stimulates the intestinal mucosal cells to release more slimy mucous. Such mucous passes in the intestine touching

ulcers.

Important Note: Those who are having low sugar level in blood should avoid taking chillies, both in food and in any type of dish.

BLACK PEPPER

On an average, black pepper contains 8.8 - 14.4 % moisture, 38-49% carbohydrates, 8-18% crude fibres, 3-6.7 % total ash, 2.5-3.6 % total nitrogen, 3.8-8.9 % piparine and pipasine. The aromatic odour is due to the presence of essential oils. Plant part used-Dried unripe fruits.

Medicinal Properties

- Boil water and place two spoonfuls of black pepper and allow it to cool. Strain and then take it to make purify water.
- Make a powder of the black pepper and place it in water. Warm it. Gargle four times a day to treat hoarseness and sore throat.
- Mix black pepper and chueb piper (Piper cubeca) in equal amount. Make a powder then take thrice a day with fresh water to cure gonorrhoea.

- Make a paste of black pepper. Apply it in the eye opposite to the site of pain on forehead to treat hemicranias.
- Make powder of black pepper. Take it inside the nostrils. Breathe gently. It will help in curing headache and to relieve sneezing.
- Make a powder of black paper and mix honey and pure ghee. Take it twice a day regularly for one month to reduce acidity.
- Grind black pepper with water to prepare a paste. Apply it on the pimples thrice a day to have a cure.
- To eliminate hay fever, crush some leaves of holy basil and black pepper and then mix them in tea. Take it thrice a day to eliminate hay fever. Mix almond without seed coat and black pepper in equal amount. Grind and then add sugar candy. Lick the mixture thrice a day to cure stammering.
- Grind black pepper and sugar candy and then mix butter. Take this mixture in the morning for one month to recover mental fatigue. Boil black pepper in milk. When milk reduces to half then cool. Take it thrice a day to treat colic pain.

CINNAMON

On an average, cinnamon contains 9.9 % moisture, 4.6 % proteins, 2.2% fat, 20.3 % fibre, 59.5 % carbohydrates, 3.5 %

total ash, 2.5 % mineral matter and vitamins B_1, B_2, C and A. Plant part used-Dried inner part of stem.

Medicinal Properties

- Take cinnamon and Bishop's seed (Trachyspermurn ammi) in equal amount. Slowly boil for three minutes in water. Strain and then take half cup in the morning and half cup in the evening. It cures fever and congestion. It also keeps cold and flu away.
- Make a powder of cinnamon. Take 2 gms twice a day with water to cure dysentery.
- Take a piece of cinnamon in mouth and chew it thoroughly before swallowing to treat stammering.
- Take 3 gms cinnamon with warm milk daily at night before sleep. It will increase the sperm count and will also promote sexual stimulation.

LONG PEPPER

Long pepper contains 11.7 % moisture, 41 % carbohydrates, 8.3 % crude fibre, 4.1 % total ash, and Vitamins B_1 B_2 ' C and A. Biting taste is due to an alkaloid, paparine. Plant part used - Dried unripe fruit.

Medicinal Properties

- Make a powder of fruits. Take one spoonful twice a day along with water to cure epilepsy.
- Boil fruits in water. When water level becomes half then strain. Take juice twice a day for one month to treat chronic bronchitis.
- Make a powder of seeds and mix it with honey in equal amount. Lick it twice a day to treat goitre.
- Mix the powder of fruit with honey. Take it at night before sleep to keep cough away.
- Make a powder of fruit and give one spoonful along with cow's milk once in a day to keep spleen fit.

NUTMEG

Nutmeg consists of 14.3 % moisture, 7.5 % proteins, 28.6% carbohydrates, 11.6 % fibre, 1.7 % mineral matter, 6.16 % nutmeg oil, 2.5% pentosans, 1.5% furfural, 0.6% pectin and vitamins B_1, B_2, C and A. Plant part used.

Medicinal Properties

- Grind seeds in water and take twice a day with the water of curd to cure dysentery.

- Rub seeds in milk to prepare a paste. Apply it over the acne and pimples on the face before sleep. Repeat it for one month to treat acne.
- Take 21 seeds and make a rosary. Place it around the neck of patient. It will keep epilepsy away.
- Rub seeds in pure ghee to prepare a paste. Apply it over the eyelids. The patient will get a sound sleep.
- Make a powder of seeds and mix it with mustard oil (Brassica campestris). Rub it over the joints to cure arthritis.
- In headache due to cold, rub a seed on the stone to make a paste. Apply it over the nostrils and forehead.
- Make a powder of seeds and mix with wine to prepare a paste. Apply it over the site of pain in joints.
- Roast seeds and mix gud. Make pills of small size. Take a pill at the interval of 10 minutes, to treat cholera.

Important Note: Excessive doses of nutmeg taken orally will produce narcotic effect causing delirium and epileptic convulsions after 1-6 hours. So, take precautions.

SMALL CARDAMOM

Cardamom seeds contain 7-10% moisture, 5 to 10% Volatile oil, 3.2 - 6.7% total ash, 6.9 to 13% crude fibre, 7 - 14% protein,

38.8 to 50.1 % carbohydrates and vitamins B_1, B_2, C and A. The seeds have a characteristic aroma due to cineol, terpineol, turpinenen, sabinene and limonene. Plant part used– Fruit and Seeds.

Medicinal Properties

- Mix seeds and sugarcandy in equal amount and grind them in the form of powder. Add the powder in pure castor oil and take it twice a day to improve eyesight.
- Take seeds and make a powder. Place the powder inside the nostrils and then, breathe gently to cure headache.
- Take husks and grind them. Boil till water reduces to one-fourth. Leave for cooling and then strain. Take half a cup several times. It will stop vomitting, quench thirst and clear urination. It is also a good formula for treating cholera.
- Mix seeds and husks of Isabgol (Plantago ovata) in equal amount. Grind them along with fresh fruits of Anola (Emblica officinalis) and make pills. Take one pill in the morning and one in the evening along with cow's milk to cure spermatorrhoea.
- Make a powder of seeds and boil in water. When water reduces to half, cool it, take twice a day to cure liver disorders.

- Make the powder of seeds and add it in curd. Take such curd twice a day for 3 days only to neutralise the poison of Jamologhota.

TAMALA

The dried leaves contain 5.7% moisture, 10.2% proteins, 20.1% fat, 15.2% crude fibre, 45% carbohydrates, 6.6% total ash, 3.1% mineral matter, vitamins B, B_2,' C and A. Leaves contain an essential oil. Plant part used-Leaves.

Medicinal properties

- Grind the leaves, and make a paste. Apply it over the inflammation of joints twice a day to treat gout.
- Use the leaves as spice in vegetables or curry. The stones in kidney or in urinary bladder will soon be broken and then, will pass out through urine.
- Take leaves regularly in vegetables, curries to minimise the intestinal gas.

INDIAN MUSTARD

On an average, seeds contain 90.6% moisture, 2.6% proteins, 0.4% fat, 4.8% carbohydrates, 1.0% crude fibre, 1.6% ash

and vitamin A and C. The seeds yield pale yellow oil. Plant part used–Seeds.

Medicinal Properties

- Grind seeds and mix with cow's urine. Take twice a day to kill intestinal worms.
- Grind seeds, sugar and black pepper (Piper nigrum L.) to form a powder. Take it twice a day with warm water to cure cow.
- Grind seeds as powder. Smell it through nostrils at the time of attack to relieve epilepsy.
- Grind seeds in cow's urine and mix with clay soil to make a paste. Apply it over the itching places on body.
- Grind seeds to powder and mix with honey. Place it above the wound and tie a clove above it for speedy recovery of wounds.
- Boil seeds and make a soft paste. Apply it over the affected tooth to cure toothache.
- Grind seeds to powder. Grind turmeric (Curcuma longa L.) and fry it. Now, mix both powders and store in a bottle. Take powder with honey twice a day to reduce the phlegm.
- Grind seeds to powder and mix powder with vinegar. Apply it over the ringworm twice a day to cure this.

- Mix powder of seeds, honey and pure ghee. Take this mixture twice a day to control asthma.
- Make a powder of seeds and mix sugar. Take this mixture twice a day to improve digestion.

ALUM

Source: It is prepared by concentrating solution of potassium sulphate and aluminium sulphate to crystallisation point. On cooling, alum is obtained. Potash alum is very common.

Medicinal Properties

- Dissolve 50 gms of alum in water to make a solution. With the help of cotton, drop it in the nostril to stop bleeding from the nose.
- Fry a small part of alum and grind it to form a powder. Divide it into seven parts. Take one part with curd daily to cure jaundice.
- Mix alum with double amount of sugarcandy. Grind them to make a powder. Divide it into 15 pieces. Take one piece daily with water of milk to relieve cough.
- Fry alum and then grind it as a powder. Place it inside abscess to heal it.

Improve Your Health With Spices

- If any part of the body is injured initially, then take powder of 3 gms alum in one glass of milk.
- Dissolve alum in fresh water to make a solution. Drinking this solution thrice a day. It will give relief to cure cholera.
- Dissolve alum in fresh water to prepare solution. Apply this solution upon palm of hand and sole of foot regularly to stop oozing of sweat from palm and sole.
- Grind alum as powder and mix with butter. Apply the mixture upon gland of piles twice a day to give relief in piles.
- After shave, rub a piece of alum with water over the face. This is a good antiseptic.

LOW CALORIE SLIMMING RECIPES

Chilled Cucumber Soup

Ingredients – 500 ml curd; 100 ml cucumber juice; 100 gm cucumber ground to pulp; 2 cloves garlic (crushed); 1 ts paste of coriander and mint, salt and pepper to taste, pinc of black rock salt (kaala namak).

Method – Blend the curd in a liquidiser. Mix in th remaining ingredients. Blend again. Serve chilled, garnishe with mint leaves.

Minty Apple Soda

Ingredients – 150 ml fresh apple juice; 1 tbsp mint juic (15 ml); 2 tbsp grape juice (30 ml.); 150 ml chilled soda crushed ice.

Method – Mix together the grape, mint and apple juice and put in a tall glass. Add crushed ice and pour soda on top lightly mix and serve immediately.

Kaala Channa Salad

Ingredients – 150 gms black channa soaked overnight, and preferably sprouted, 10 gms (1 large) capsicum cut very fine, 50 gms of onion finely chopped, 2 green chillies finely sliced, 50 gms tomato finely chopped, 1/2 cup finely cut green coriander, 100 gms cucumber finely cut, 1 tsp black rock salt (kaala namak), plain salt to taste 1/2 tsp freshly ground black pepper, 1 tbsp lemon juice.

Method – Boil the soaked or sprouted channa, with 1 tsp. salt till tender. Drain and set aside to cook. Mix in the chopped onions, cucumber, tomatoes, chillies, coriander and lemon juice. Mix together the chaat masala, kala namak, plain salt, and black pepper. Sprinkle over the salad and toss well. Serve garnished with onion and tomato slices.

Chilly Garlic Chutney

Ingredients – 1 cup coriander leaves roughly chopped; 4 green chillies; 4 flakes of garlic; 1 tsp lemon juice; 2 tbsp curd; salt to taste; 1/2 cup tender green leaves of spring onion.

Method – Clean, chop and grind all the ingredients to a fine paste. You can store it in the fridge for 4-5 days.

Baked Papris

Ingredients – 100 gms whole wheat flour (atta); 2 (30 gms.) tbsp semolina (suji); 1 tbsp oil; 1/2 tbsp Bishop's weed seeds; 1 tsp curd; warm water to knead the dough.

Method – Mix together wheat flour, semolina, salt and Bishop's weed. Rub in the oil and curd with your finger tips. Knead it into stiff dough using a little warm water. Set the dough aside for 30 minutes covered with a damp clot. Make small balls from the dough and roll out as thinly as possible. Cut our round papris with a cutter or with the lid of a bottle at least 2" in diameter.

Crispy Canapies

Ingredients – 4 slices bread; 2 tbsp green chutney; 1 tbsp tomato ketchup; 1 tbsp grated carrot; 1/2 tsp chilli galic spread.

Method – Trim and cut each bread slice into 4 square pieces. Mix together the tomato ketchup, grated carrot and chilli garlic paste in a bowl. Spread green chutney over half the pieces and red ketchup mixture on the remaining pieces.

Grill in a pre-heated oven or grill till crisp (5-7 min.) Serve immediately with drinks or soup.

Tomato Orange Drink

Ingredients - 4 medium tomatoes (200 gms.); 2 orange peeled and dressed; 2-3 basil or mint leaves. 1/2" piece of ginger and a pinch of salt to taste.

Method - Wash and cut tomatoes into quarters; clean and peal the orange, wash the basil/mint leaves. Peel and wash ginger. Extract juice of all the ingredients together through a juicer. Add a pinch of salt and serve immediately in a tall grass, garnished with a small spring of basil and a wedge of orange or tomato.

•••

• *tbsp - Table Spoonfull* • *tsp - Tea Spoonfull.*

DIET CURE AND RECIPES FOR HIGH B.P. PATIENTS

RECIPES FOR HIGH B.P.

Parval Delight

Ingredients – Parval 250 gms (cut into 8 pieces length -wise) Oil - 1 tea spoon, cumin seed seeds-1/2 tea spoon, Red chili powder - 1/2 tea spoon, Salt-1/2 tea spoon, Coriander Patti 50 gms. Amchoor powder 1 tea spoon or lime juice from medium sized fruit.

Method – Add the oil + 25 ml. of water in the non stick pan and all the requirements and toss the contents making sure everything has thoroughly mixed with the parval. Place the lid and cook in low sim flame stirring the contents every minutes till 15 minutes, when the parval has been cooked and no moisture is left in the pan. Garnish with Coriander patti and serve.

Mixed Vegetable Korma

Ingredients –

Cauliflower	200 gms
Pea seeds	100 gms
Carrot discs (rounds)	100 gms
Cabbage chopped into rice	200 gms
Beet grated	100 gms (made from skimmed milk)
Coriander leaves	5-6
Onions	200 gms
Garlic	2 pods
Ginger	a small piece.

Grind them together, (onions, garlic and ginger).

Tomatoes	200 gms or 100 gms
Oil	1 tea spoon
Turmeric	½ tea spoon
Green chilli	3 long little quantity as per preference chopped into small pieces.
Coriander leaves	chopped to be added last.
Salt	½ tea spoonful.

Improve Your Health With Spices

Cardamoms	2
Cloves	5
Dalchini	few small pieces– to be ground together and added just before removing from the Flame.
Posta seeds	2 tea spoonful to be ground into a paste and added in the beginning.

Method – In a non stick pan, add 1 tea spoon of oil and 100 ml. of water thoroughly. Shake so that the oil and water form an amalgam. Then, add all the spices, shake again and add the cut vegetables except tomatoes or tomato puree. Shake well and cover the lid, heat in low flame for 10-15 minutes, when the vegetables have been semi-cooked, add the puree or chopped tomatoes and again cover and heat for 5 minutes.

At last, add the chopped coriander leaves and garam masala, toss the contents and it is ready to be served.

Jack Fruit (Kathal Curry)

Cauliflower	200 gms
Kathal	250 gms (peal and cut into small pieces after applying oil on the knife).
Onions	200 gms

Improve Your Health With Spices

Ginger	a small piece (Ground)
Garlic	2 pods
Saunf seeds	50 gms roast and grind
Turmeric powder	½ tea spoon
Red chilli powder	½ tea spoon
Salt	1 tea spoon
Coriander leaves	few
Tomatoes	200 gms cut into pieces
Garam masala	1 tea spoon
Oil	1 tea spoon

Method – Steam the small cut pieces of Kathal till half cooked and place the pieces aside in a non-stick pan. Add a tea spoonful oil and 200 ml water, shake well to mix the two. Then, add garam masala and pieces of Kathal and shake well and heat in low flame for 15 minutes. Then, add the chopped tomatoes or puree + coriander leaves + garam masala and heat for 5 minutes. By now, the pieces of Kathal will be soft and ready to be served.

Bitter gourd Curry
Ingredients-

Cauliflower	200 gms
Bitter gourd	200 gms.

Tamarind	50 gms soaked in water
Fennel seeds	50 gms roast and grind.
Turmeric	½ tea spoon
Red chilli powder	1 tea spoon
Salt	1 tea spoon
Green Coriander	few patti chopped
Sugar or any Jam	2 table spoonful

Method – Steam the scraped cut pieces of bitter gourd till 75% cooked. Wash in water and leave to strain the water off. Take a non-stick pans add 1 tea spoon oil + 100 ml water + tamarind paste + salt + fennel + turmeric + chilli powder and mix the mixture with the steamed pieces of bitter gourd and cover the lid and cook for 10 minutes with the lid on, in low flame. Then, remove the lid and add the sugar crystals or Jam of Pineapple and again heat for 5 minutes. Then, add the coriander patti and serve hot.

Khatta-Mitha Egg Plant Curry
Ingredients–

Egg plants	long cut into 2 pieces
each with a slith	length wise - 4 pieces
Fennel	50 gms roasted and grounded.

Turmeric	½ tea spoonful
Salt	1 tea spoonful
Chilli powder	1 tea spoon
Coriander	Few
Onion	200 gms
Ginger	25 gms
Garlic	2 pods grind the masala
Tamarind	100 gms soak and make a paste.
Sugar or Jam (Pine apple or mango)	2 table spoonful. Steam the egg plants till cooked and leave aside.

Method – In the non-stick pan, add all the masala in 1 tea spoon of oil + 100 ml of water for 10 minutes in low flame after covering the lid. Then, remove the lid and slowly heat the steamed egg plant pieces in the pan so that they may not break into a lump, cover the lid and heat for 5-7 minutes again so that the masala gravy penetrates in the pieces. Add the coriander leaves and the dish is ready to be served.

Nav Ratan Kari of gram-flour
Ingredients–

Yoghurt	250 gms (of skimmed milk)
Besan / black gram flour	100 gms

Carrots/Radish	50 gms (cut into diagonal discs cut length wise).
French beans	50 gms (cut into small pieces)
Turnip	50 gms (cut into small pieces)
Pointed gourd	25 gms (cut into long pieces)
Onions	circularly cut
Coriander leaves	a few chopped
Fenugreek seeds	½ tea spoon
Magrela seeds	½ tea spoon
Cumin seeds	½ tea spoon
Asafoetida	a little
Red Chilli Powder	1 tea spoon
Mustard Seeds	½ tea spoon.

Tip : For the success Yoghurt must be a little sour (about 2-3 days old) – churn it properly and mix the 100 gms gram powder into it thoroughly. Add salt, turmeric and red chilli powder and keep aside, at the end add 500 ml water to it.

Method – In a wok roast the above-mentioned ingredients dry, add 1 tea spoon of oil to it - heat it and then add the Yoghurt mixture to it and boil.

On the other side steam all the cut vegetables till they turn

Improve Your Health With Spices

semi-soft and transfer the steamed vegetables into the boiling mixture of Yoghurt gram powder slowly so that the vegetables pieces do not break.

Let the mixture boil twice and add the coriander leaves and remove from flame. The nav ratan curry is ready.

Mushroom Tomato Curry

Ingredients-

Mushroom buttons	250 gms.
Tomatoes	500 gms. / 2 Cups of purie.
Onion	200 gms.
Ginger	25 gms.
Salt	1 tea spoon
Turmeric	½ tea spoon
Red chilli powder	½ tea spoon
Curry patta or 2 bay leaves	
Oil	1 tea spoon
Garam masala	1 tea Spoon
Raisins	50 gms

Cut the mushroom into small pieces and place aside.

Method – In a non-stick pan, place roasted seeds of fenugreek, cumin seed and mustard seeds + 1 tea spoon oil + bay leaves or curry patta + salt + turmeric + red chilli powder + tomatoes or puree, cover the lid and cook for 10 minutes. Then, open the lid and transfer the cut pieces of mushroom + garam masala and cook for 5 minutes. A few pieces of raisins or even grapes may be added just before removing from fire.

Nawabi Phoolgobhi Curry (Cauliflower)
Ingredients–

Yoghurt	100 gms (from skimmed milk)
Cauliflower	250 gms
Tomatoes	200 gms or 1 cup puree
Onions	200 gms
Ginger	25 gms
Grinded Garlic	2 pods
Salt	1 tea spoon
Turmeric	1 tea spoon
Red chilli powder	½ tea spoon
Asafoetida	a little
Cashew nuts & Raisins	50 gms each grinded into paste.
Coriander leaves	a few

Curry patta / bay leaves	2
Garam masala powder	½ tea spoon
Oil	1 tea spoon.

Method – In a non-stick pan place 1 tea spoon of oil+100 ml water and add all the masala. Then, add the cut pieces of cauliflower (after washing it thoroughly) into it and toss the contents till everything mixes well. Place the lid and heat for 10 minutes in low flame. Then, add the tomato chopped pieces or puree. Again heat for 7 minutes in low flame. By now the cauliflower will be soft and cooked. Then, add the garam masala and remove from flame. Add the coriander leaves and serve hot.

Boiled peas can also be added to the above dish.

Germinated Seeds Dal
Ingredients–

Any whole grains can be kept moist and germinated

The germinated seeds	200 gms
Onions chopped	100 gms
Garlic	2 pods
Tomatoes	100 gms
Ginger	10 gms

Salt	1 tea spoon
Turmeric	½ tea spoon
Red chilli powder or chopped green chilli	little.
Garam masala	½ tea spoon
Roasted seeds of fenugreek (fenugreek) cumin (cumin seeds)	½ tea spoon each
Vegetable oil	1 tea spoon.

Method – Place the above mentioned ingredients in a non-stick pan in 1 tea spoon oil + 50 ml. water and heat in low flame for 10 minutes. Then, add the chopped tomatoes and heat for 5 minutes. Add the garam masala and serve hot.

Fruits like plantain, orange slices, apple discs or papaya can lend flavour or taste to it.

•••

DIET CURE FOR HYPERTENSION

Rest and relaxation are of utmost importance during the period of specific diet. The regulated diet period for hypertension can be from five to fifteen days. It is better to start with five days initially. During this period, absolute normalcy is usually attained, after which just by avoiding certain items from diet and with mild exercises and relaxation one can lead a normal life.

Calcium and potassium are the two essential nutrients necessary to expel excess sodium, which is harmful in hypertension. Dairy products are rich in calcium in its natural form. Fruits and vegetables contain a good quantity of potassium.

The following diet schedule should be adhered to for seven days—

5:30 a.m. : Juice of one lemon and two teaspoon honey, added to a glass of water extracted from wheat soaked previous morning.

6:30 a.m.	: Juice extracted from 2 big onions and 2-3 cloves of garlic.
9:30 a.m.	: Juice of seasonal vegetables, such as, cucumber, carrots, tomatoes and bottle gourd in which juice of six Indian hog plum and ginger should be added (juice can be extracted from any one or all the above vegetables).
11:00 a.m.	: Two rotis made of old wheat, one bowl boiled vegetables with very little salt, if you find salt less food unpalatable. One bowl sprouted pulses, one bowl curd.
12:30 p.m.	: One big glass of buttermilk (without salt).
2:30 p.m.	: Seasonal fruits, such as orange, watermelon and other juicy fruits.
4:30 p.m.	: One glass of vegetable juice made out of seasonal vegetables.
7.30 p.m	: Seasonal fruit, such as, pears, sapodilla, jamun, raspberry, melons, sweet lime apples, guavas, pineapple, etc. After the initial seven days more items can be included.

Are you reluctant to avoid salt due to the fear of becoming weak? Do not loose heart. Even, if there is no control in the salt

Improve Your Health With Spices

intake, the incidence of hypertension is low in persons who consume potassium in the form of fresh vegetable and fruits. But, be wise and at least reduce its intake considerably and gradually stop it altogether.

To lower the blood pressure, one more valuable substance is garlic. Garlic has the quality of relaxing the spasm of the blood vessels. It also eases the shortness of breath and gas formation in the digestive tract. It slows down the pulse and normalises the rhythm of heart. Two cloves of garlic per day help to maintain normal blood pressure.

•••

MAGIC OF WATER

Once, an old Japanese man enjoyed a perfect health. He was once met by a curious professor. When asked about the secret of his robust condition, the old man explained that it was due to water. He went on to tell in detail about his sickly youth, when he was bed-ridden, with impaired intestines, for almost ten years. When all the modes of treatment failed to bring even partial relief from his sickness, he was told it was impossible to get a cure. One of the physicians who treated him, however, suggested a specific type of water treatment as a last resort.

The effect of the treatment was felt on the very first day and his appetite was restored, his digestion improved and within a few days he was cured of his chronic disease. It might have been a coincidence, that the treatment he underwent all those years showed results only after this simple water treatment. So, impressed with this treatment was he, that he tried it on the members of his family who were suffering from various illnesses ranging from brain fever to obesity and achieved positive results.

What is the water magic?

The process is as follows– Go to sleep three hours after a fairly early dinner around 7.00 p.m. Strictly do not eat or drink anything after that. Rise early from bed the next morning, do not wash your face and mouth as you do normally. Sit comfortably and drink six glasses of pure water at a stretch. If you find difficulty in doing so, pause a while after two or three glasses and continue. For the next 20 minutes walk briskly or do some exercise. Within twenty minutes to half an hour, urge to pass urine will be great and you will pass urine in large quantities quite frequently. Some may bring out the morbid waste through vomiting. Passing of stools will be easy and complete. It will facilitate the expulsion of the accumulated waste matter very effectively and leave you fresh.

•••

NARCOTICS / SMOKING / ALCOHOL / AGEING NARCOTICS

- Alcohol is a drug, make no mistake about it.
- Current evidence suggests that, moderate drinking won't hurt us, unless we are allergic to alcohol or have a tendency to alcoholism.
- Statistics suggest that, light drinking decreases our long-range risk of heart attacks.
- All reports demonstrate that, chronic heavy drinking can result in chronic gastrointestinal malfunction as well as extensive organ damage to the liver, pancreas, heart and brain.
- Illegal drugs such as, marijuana, cocaine, heroin, and others are all considered bad for us, though heroin is regarded as the most toxic and addictive, as well as, the most menacing to other members of society, while of those mentioned marijuana is the least harmful.

- Using these drugs will make you to age faster.
- Just thinking about the possibility of getting busted by the authorities for possession of these illegal substances is enough to add a few gray hairs to your head.
- Cut down on your alcohol intake. The more alcohol consumed, the more problematic sex becomes. Alcohol lowers the testosterone level in men, creating potency problems. In women, it delays orgasm.
- Add more zinc to your diet. Zinc is helpful in the maintenance to male sexual health and vigour, according to Georgetown University researchers. Smoking and drinking depletes our ability to use zinc, liver, sunflower, seeds, oats, nuts, and cheese are good sources of zinc.
- Exercise regularly, the more active you are, the greater will be your vigour and interest in sex, both mentally and physically.

SMOKING

- One fact that, the public sometimes misses is that the major cause of decreased life expectancy as a result of smoking cigarettes is not cancer; it is heart disease. .

- Some interesting longevity conclusions made from recent studies regarding smoking are given below -
  -Smokers die faster than non-smokers, at every age and with the increased number of cigarettes smoked and smokers die at a greater rate from every disease.
  - Non-smoking wives or husbands of cigarette smokers have lowered life expectancy.
  - One–pack-a-day smokers have twice the chance of nonsmokers of dying from age fifty to sixty. Two–pack-a-day smokers have thrice the chance.
  - On an average, smokers die about eight years younger than non-smokers.

ALCOHOL

Alcohol increases HDL-C levels in some patients, but it also considerably increases their plasma TG levels.

Alcohol should be eliminated because of inherent problems, as well as, its effects on TG, especially in those with already high TG levels. Alcohol use to raise HDL levels is not recommended. (TG- Triglycerides)

Moreover, alcohol is an additional source of calories. Each ml contains 7 calories. It is also known to exacerbate neuropathy,

lipidaemia, obesity and control of diabetes. It can prevent a person from following proper diabetes management and from recognising the symptoms of hypoglycaemia till, it is too late.

TIPS TO SLOW DOWN AGING

- Take foods rich in zinc.
- Take egg plant, yogurt and onions frequently to combat cholesterol.
- Take apples and citrus fruit often and supplement the diet with soybean lecithin to fight cholesterol.
- Drink an extra 8 ounce glass of water each day.

•••

CALORIES, HEIGHT-WEIGHT & ESSENTIAL NUTRIENTS TABLES

Table of Calories Burnt in Physical Activities

In the following table, an effort has been made to figure out calories burnt by an individual in relation to his/her physical activity (For all sexes age - groups).

Activity	Calories expended per hour
(i) Light Activity	**50-200 Calories Group**
Lying down / sleeping	80
Sitting	100
Driving a Car	120
Household work	180
(ii) Moderate Activity	**200-300 Calories Group**
Bicycling (8.25 kms)	210
Walking (4.25 kms)	210

	Gardening	220
	Canoeing (4.25 kms)	230
	Golf	250
	Lawn-Mowing (Power Mover)	250
	Lawn-Mowing (Hand Mover)	270
	Bowling	270
(iii)	**Marked Activity**	**300-400 Calories Group**
	Walking (6 kms)	300
	Swimming (40 mtrs.)	300
	Rowing (4.25 kms)	300
	Fencing	300
	Badminton	350
	Horse-Riding (Trotting)	350
	Roller-Skating	350
	Volleyball	350
	Square Dancing	350
	Table-Tennis	360
(iv)	**Vigorous Activity**	**Over 400 Calories Group**
	Ice-skating (16 kms)	400
	Sawing or wood-chopping	400
	Tennis	420

Hill-climbing	480
Skiing	490
Handball	600
Bicycling (21 kms)	600
Running (16 kms)	900

Table of Daily Calorie Requirements
(during 24 hours)

Age Group	Calorie Requirements
upto 6 months body weight	120 Calories per kg
7-12 months body weight	100 Calories per kg
1-3 years	1200 Calories
4-6 years	1500 Calories
7-9 years	1800 Calories
10-12 years	2100 Calories
13-15 years (boys)	2500 Calories
13-15 years (girls)	2200 Calories
16-18 years (boys)	3000 Calories
16-18 years (girls)	2200 Calories
Men, doing light work	2200 Calories

Men, doing medium work	2800 Calories
Men, doing heavy work	3400 Calories
Women, doing light work	1900 Calories
Women, doing medium work	2200 Calories
Women, doing heavy work	2800 Calories

Note - Parameters shown above are merely indicative of general standards but calories for each person is required to be worked out on the basis of age, sex, amount of manual labour put in, health status, person's height, weight and climate of a place.

Daily Calorie According to Body Weight and Activity
(Daily Calorie Requirement in Food)

(Per kg Body Weight)

Weight	Office Workers (Light Work)	Medium work	Hard Work
Under weight	35	40	45
Normal weight	30	35	40
Overweight	20	25	30

Note: For Athletes, sportspersons, persons engaged in strenuous work, children in growth period, pregnant women and man with malnutrition, calorie requirement should be measured in relation to physical condition and the amount of calories expended or

expected to be spent. Each case has, naturally, to be individualised because no two cases could be identical. Since, weight also must commensurate with height of a person and, in keeping with requirements of these two factors, the following table will give an idea as to whether a person's weight is in proportion to his height.

Table of Ideal Body Weight in Kgs. and Height in Cms

Height (in cms)	Weight (in kgs)			
	18-20 yrs	23-27 yrs	28-32 yrs	33-37 yrs
150	45.5	47.0	48.3	49.4
152	46.2	47.8	49.7	50.4
154	47.1	48.7	50.3	51.4
156	48.0	49.7	51.4	52.6
158	49.5	50.8	52.5	53.7
160	50.0	52.0	53.7	54.9
162	51.2	53.2	54.9	56.1
164	52.4	54.4	56.2	57.2
166	53.7	55.7	57.6	59.0
168	55.1	57.2	59.9	60.0

170	56.5	58.7	60.6	62.2
172	58.2	60.2	62.1	63.9
174	59.5	61.7	63.7	65.6
176	61.0	63.3	65.3	67.3
178	62.5	64.9	67.0	69.00
180	64.1	66.5	68.7	70.7
182	65.7	68.1	70.4	72.4
184	67.3	69.7	72.1	74.1
186	68.9	71.4	73.8	75.8
188	70.5	73.1	75.6	77.8
190	72.1	74.8	77.4	79.6

Height (in cms)	Weight (in kgs)			
	38-42 yrs	43-47 yrs	48-52 yrs	above 53 yrs
150	49.8	50.1	50.3	50.5
152	50.8	51.1	51.3	51.5
154	51.9	52.2	52.4	52.1
156	53.0	53.3	53.6	53.7
158	54.1	54.4	54.7	54.9
160	55.3	55.7	56.0	56.3
162	56.6	57.0	57.4	57.7

164	58.0	58.5	58.9	59.2
166	59.5	60.0	60.4	60.8
168	61.1	61.6	62.0	62.4
170	62.8	63.2	63.7	64.1
172	64.5	65.0	65.5	65.9
174	66.2	66.7	67.3	67.7
176	67.9	68.4	69.1	69.5
178	69.6	70.2	70.9	71.3
180	71.3	72.0	72.9	73.2
182	73.0	73.8	74.5	75.1
184	74.8	75.6	76.3	77.0
186	76.6	77.4	78.1	78.9
188	78.4	79.2	79.9	80.8
190	80.2	81.0	81.7	82.7

Note: ± 5% weight should be taken as normal weight or, to be precise, marginally high/average weight. But ± 15-20 % weight, over and above the ideal weight, should be considered as 'overweight' and the latter calls for a guarded and modified approach in tapering and slashing down calories but care should be taken that calories, are not reduced to such an extent that a person gets weaker and is not in a fit frame to discharge even his normal chores.

Table of Daily Average Requirement of Essential Nutrients

Vitamins		Daily Requirement
Vitamin 'A'	(For Normal Person)	5000 I.U.
	(For Pregnant Women)	8000 I.U.
B_1 (Thiamine)		1.25 mg
B_2 (Riboflavin)		1.50 mg
B_6 (Pyridoxine)		2.00 mg
B_{12} (Cobalamin)		6.00 mg
Niacin (Nictoinamide)		20 mg
B_5 (Pentatonic Acid)		10 mg
Botanic and Folic acid		0.31 mg
Vitamin -C (Ascorbic Acid)		60 mg
Vitamin - D (Calciferol)		400 - I.U.
Vitamin - E (Tocopherol)		30 I.U. - 400 I.U.
Vitamin - F		Not clear
Vitamin - K (depending on clotting condition)		S.O.S.
Vitamin - P (Bioflavonoid)		Not clear

Minerals and Trace Elements

Calcium	For growing children	500-800 mg
Calcium	For Nursing / Lactating Mothers	1000-1400 mg
Calcium	For Adults	400-500 mg
Chromium		1-2 mg
Copper		2 mg
Iron		12-15 mg
Iodine		.01 - .02 mg
Manganese		5 mg
Magnesium		200-400 mg
Phosphorus		1 mg
Potassium		1000-4000 mgm (1-4 gms)
Sodium		400-1500 mgm
Selenium		50-200 mgm
Zinc		10-15 mg

Note: In short, all efforts should be made to derive energy from available natural sources, such as vegetables, sea-foods (including fish), grain cereals, natural water resources, animal foods & products (like milk, butter, clarified butter, cheese, whey etc.), poultry products. As far as possible, try to avoid branded and commercial products and medicines, tinned and exposed foods, etc. Emphasis ought to be on the quality of the food, but never on the quantity.

•••

Glossary of Hindi Terms

Gud	—	Jaggery
Munakka	—	Raisins
Dalchini	—	Cinnamon
Mishri	—	Rock candy, large crystallized sugar also known as rock sugar
Ilaichi	—	Cardamom
Laddoo	—	Round sweetmeat
Suji	—	Semolina
Mung ki Dal	—	Mung bean dal
Dhania	—	Coriander
Sonth	—	Dried ginger
Gulabjal	—	The rose water
Saunf	—	Fennel
Kheer	—	Indian rice pudding
Isabgol	—	Laxative
Kaala Channa	—	Black Gram
Parval	—	Pointed gourd
Kathal	—	Jackfruit
Roti	—	Thin rounds of unleavened bread
Jamun	—	Small purple fruit with a big stone, sweet-sour in flavour
Khaskhas	—	Poppy seeds

Diamond Pocket Books presents
NEW COOKERY SERIES

Dr. Bimal Chhajer

Zero Oil Cook Book 150.00
Zero Oil Namkeen (151 Snacks) 150.00
Zero Oil Sweets Book 150.00
Zero Oil South Indian Cook Book 150.00

Neera Verma

Rice Cook Book 100.00
Dry, Stuffed, Juicy, Vegetable................95.00
Paneer Cook Book.................................95.00

Tahlina Kaul

Indian Microwave Cook Book...............100.00
Non-Vegetarian Cook Book 100.00
Vegetarian Cook Book 100.00

Neera Verma

Indian Cook Book 45.00
Vegetarian Cook Book 45.00
Chinese Cook Book 35.00
South Indian Cook Book 35.00
Breakfast Specialities 35.00
Pickles, Chutneys, Jams........................35.00

Soups Cook Book 35.00
Cakes, Pastries, Pudding 35.00
Ice Creams, Cakes, Pudding 45.00
Fruit Drinks, Juices, Cordials................45.00
Delicious Indian Sweets 35.00
Gujarati Cook Book................................35.00
Non-Vegetarian Cook Book 45.00
Punjabi Cook Book 35.00
Mughlai Cook Book................................45.00

Neena Puri

Paneer Hungama (Cook Book) 45.00
Paneer Khazana (Cook Book) 45.00
Paneer Magic (Cook Book) 45.00

Books can be requisitioned by V.P.P. Postage charges will be Rs. 20/- per book. For orders of three books the postage will be free.

✺ DIAMOND BOOKS

X-30, Okhla Industrial Area, Phase-II, New Delhi-110020, Phone : 011-51611861, Fax : 011-51611866
E-mail info@diamondpublication.com, Website: www.diamondpublication.com

FUSION BOOKS PRESENTS

A series of Zero Oil Books & Health Tips by Dr. Bimal Chhajer, M.D.

In the hectic world of today, man's life is full of stress and strains and his life is always under pressure. Many times, besides the strains, diets full of oils and fats also cause several diseases. Hence, we have to curtail or reduce the intake of oils in our diet. For this the best method is Zero Oil recipes. Zero oil cuisines are equally tasty and healthy as any other. Now, do you need oil or taste?

201 Tips for Losing Weight... 150/-

201 Tips for Diabetes Patients... 150/-

201 Diet Tips for Heart Patients... 150/-

Zero Oil Thali... 150/-

Zero Oil Cook Book... 150/-

Zero Oil Sweets Book... 150/-

South Indian Cook Book... 150/-

Zero Oil 151 Snacks Namkeen... 150/-

Books can be requisitioned by V.P.P. Postage charges will be Rs. 20/- per book. For orders of three books the postage will be free.

◎ DIAMOND BOOKS

X-30, Okhla Industrial Area, Phase-II, New Delhi-110020, Phone : 011-51611861, Fax : 011-51611866
E-mail info@diamondpublication.com, Website: www.diamondpublication.com